Rivers, Lakes, and Marshes

THIS EDITION
Editorial Management by Oriel Square
Produced for DK by WonderLab Group LLC
Jennifer Emmett, Erica Green, Kate Hale, *Founders*

Editors Grace Hill Smith, Libby Romero, Maya Myers, Michaela Weglinski;
Photography Editors Kelley Miller, Annette Kiesow, Nicole DiMella; **Managing Editor** Rachel Houghton;
Designers Project Design Company; **Researcher** Michelle Harris; **Copy Editor** Lori Merritt;
Indexer Connie Binder; **Proofreader** Larry Shea; **Reading Specialist** Dr. Jennifer Albro;
Curriculum Specialist Elaine Larson

Published in the United States by DK Publishing
1745 Broadway, 20th Floor, New York, NY 10019

Copyright © 2023 Dorling Kindersley Limited
DK, a Division of Penguin Random House LLC
23 24 25 26 10 9 8 7 6 5 4 3 2 1
001-334123-Sept/2023

A catalog record for this book
is available from the Library of Congress.
HC ISBN: 978-0-7440-7559-5
PB ISBN: 978-0-7440-7560-1

DK books are available at special discounts when purchased in bulk for sales promotions, premiums,
fundraising, or educational use. For details, contact: DK Publishing Special Markets,
1745 Broadway, 20th Floor, New York, NY 10019
SpecialSales@dk.com

Printed and bound in China

The publisher would like to thank the following for their kind permission to reproduce their images:
a=above; c=center; b=below; l=left; r=right; t=top; b/g=background

123RF.com: 1xpert 6tl, alzam 19cr, madllen 28bl, Aleksandr Papichev 19tr, yobro10 35tr; **Dorling Kindersley:** Thomas Marent 20b,
Nigel Hicks 18-19, Sofian Moumene / NOAA: Earth Observatory / ETOPO1 / NOAA. 20tl; **Dreamstime.com:** Akinshin 14tl,
Mihai Andritoiu 36tl, Anirootboom1326 23tr, Antares614 12-13, Antartis 12t, ArtDesignWorks 8-9, Atovot 32tl, Beehler 6-7,
Bethel7019 32-33, Blueringmedia 10tl, Bonita Cheshier / Bonniemarie 25crb, Dreamshot 21bl, Maria Luisa Lopez Estivill 26tl,
Bonnie Fink 37tr, Astrid Gast 36-37, Honourableandbold 29tr, Iofoto 40b, Janedbal 34-35, Jocrebbin 38-39, Paula Joyce 42tl,
Justoomm 33tr, Iuliia Kuzenkova 25t, Paul Lemke / Lokinthru 31crb, Joao Luis / Joaoluis 27tr, Meinzahn 42clb, Miceking 18tl,
MrLis 36clb, Dmitry Naumov 3cb, Bill O'Neill 39tr, Okea 41cr, Ava Peattie 30tl, Photophreak 28-29, Porojnicu 4-5, Sabellopro 13tr,
Sekarb 22cla, Joe Sohm 8cl, Anton Starikov 23cr, David Steele 15tl, Andrey Tarantin 26-27, VectorMine 15crb, Verastuchelova 34tl,
Chia-ling Yeh 42-43, Maksim Zabarovskii 30-31; **Getty Images:** Colors and shapes of underwater world 22-23, Michele Falzone 17tr,
Jackal Pan 41t; **Getty Images / iStock:** 4nadia 16-17, FrankRamspott 7tr, johnny123 24br, primeimages 45tr, Jennifer_Sharp 43tr,
Rafael_Wiedenmeier 24tl; **Shutterstock.com:** Goran_Safarek 26cl

Cover images: *Front:* **Getty Images / iStock:** Fabian Gysel

All other images © Dorling Kindersley
For more information see: www.dkimages.com

For the curious
www.dk.com

Level
4

Rivers, Lakes, and Marshes

Jen Szymanski

CONTENTS

Hydrosphere
The prefix "hydro-" means "water." The hydrosphere is all of the water on Earth. Scientists who study the hydrosphere are called hydrologists.

EARTH'S WATER

It's a warm spring day in the Canadian province of Ontario. The Sun shines brightly on a high hilltop, making the snow that covers the ground glisten and sparkle. By midmorning, the snow starts to melt. A single drop of water begins to slide down the slope of the hill. It is soon followed by another water drop—and then another.

By noon, water from melting snow is flowing in a steady trickle. It crosses the path of another thin stream of snowmelt, and widens. The stream empties into another larger stream and then flows into Lake Nipigon, the largest lake inside Ontario's borders.

But the water's journey is far from over. From there, it moves first into Lake Superior and then into the other Great Lakes. The tiny drop of water is now part of the largest group of lakes in the world.

From Lake to Ocean Water from the Great Lakes eventually empties into the Atlantic Ocean.

A Good Nickname
One of Earth's nicknames is "the big, blue marble." Can you see why?

Limnology
Scientists that study lakes, rivers, and other bodies of water are called limnologists. The prefix "limno–" means "marshy" or "fresh water."

The picture above shows Earth from space. The blue parts of the photo are water. You can even see the Great Lakes.

There's a lot of water on Earth! In fact, about 70 percent of Earth's surface is covered with water. It all adds up to trillions and trillions of gallons of water.

Most living things, including people, need fresh water to survive. Surprisingly, though, there's not very much fresh water to go around.

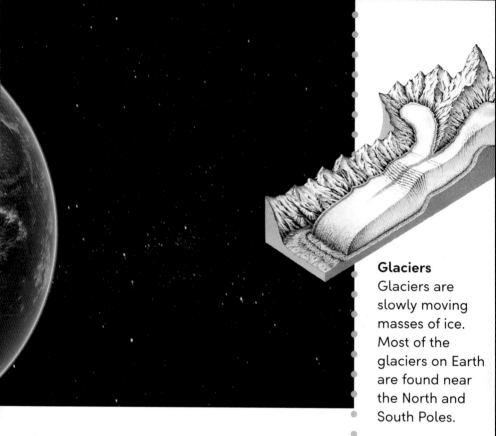

Glaciers
Glaciers are slowly moving masses of ice. Most of the glaciers on Earth are found near the North and South Poles.

Nearly all of the water on Earth—97 percent—is ocean water. Ocean water is salty.

Less than three percent of the water on Earth is fresh water. And two-thirds of that is ice. It's frozen in glaciers or locked in the ice caps located at our planet's North and South Poles. About one percent of Earth's water is fresh liquid that living things can use.

Don't Be Salty
Salt water is filled with the same white substance that fills your kitchen shaker—salt!

Transpiration
A plant's roots take in water. The water travels through the plant. Then, it evaporates from the plant's leaves. This is called transpiration.

Think about the last time you had a nice cool drink of water. That water was fresh, but it most assuredly wasn't new! The water you drink is so old that it might have once carried a pharaoh's barge in Egypt or fallen as rain on a dinosaur egg! All of Earth's water is constantly moving and being recycled over and over again through a process called the water cycle.

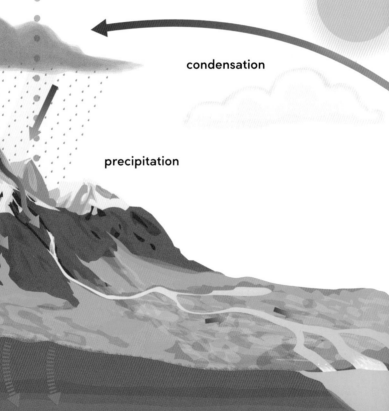

condensation

precipitation

The water cycle is driven by energy from the Sun. The Sun's rays strike liquid water on Earth's surface, warming it and causing it to change into water vapor. Water evaporates, or changes from a liquid to a gas. The water vapor rises high into the sky. The temperature is much cooler above Earth, so the water vapor condenses, or changes from a gas back to a liquid. When this happens, we see the tiny drops of water as clouds, mist, or fog.

ice

liquid water

steam

Water in Different Forms
Everything in the universe is made of matter. Matter often takes one of three forms, or states: solid, liquid, or gas. Ice and snow are solids. Rain is a liquid. Steam and water vapor are gases.

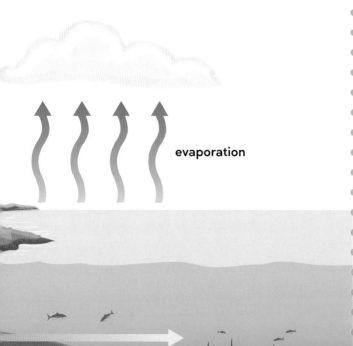

evaporation

How Long?
Water usually stays in rivers and streams for 12 to 20 days before it evaporates. But it often stays in the ocean for thousands of years before moving on in the water cycle.

Up in the sky, tiny droplets of water start to stick together. They form larger and larger drops. Eventually, the drops become too large and heavy to stay in the sky and they fall to the ground. Water that falls from the sky is called precipitation. Usually, it is in the form of rain or snow.

Once water reaches the ground, it stays on the move. Some water falls in the ocean and immediately becomes salt water. Some water becomes part of Earth's freshwater system of streams, rivers, lakes, and marshes. Some water sinks into the ground, where it becomes part of the groundwater supply or is absorbed by plants. And some water falls in warm places and collects in shallow puddles. Here, the water evaporates almost immediately and starts the water cycle all over again.

Precipitation
Meteorologists are scientists who study weather. They have names for precipitation. In addition to rain, snow, sleet, and hail, they also use the terms "drizzle" (a light rain) and "graupel" (soft hail or snow pellets).

Flying Jellybeans
Pictures usually show raindrops shaped like teardrops. But raindrops are really shaped like flattened jellybeans or hamburger buns.

Headwater
Sometimes, a stream that is the source of a river is called a headwater.

RIVERS

Every continent on Earth has at least one river. Each of Earth's rivers is unique, but all rivers have some things in common.

All rivers have a starting point called a source. Some rivers start from springs that bubble up from beneath the ground. The water in the springs comes from rain that soaks through soil and joins groundwater below the surface.

Other rivers start with runoff, or water that flows on the surface. Runoff comes from melting ice or snow and precipitation that doesn't soak into the ground. This water travels from higher ground to lower ground. It is pulled downhill by the force of gravity.

Upstream, Downstream
The direction going toward a river's source is called upstream. The direction moving away from its source is called downstream.

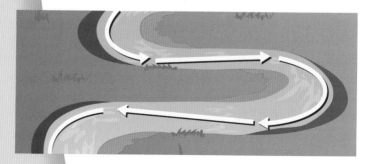

Stream Names
Around the world, people have lots of names for streams. In different places, streams are called creeks, rills, burns, races, backwaters, and brooks.

When runoff travels the same path over and over, it can form a groove in the ground. As it flows, the water picks up pieces of soil and grit. This process is called erosion. Over time, the force of erosion causes the groove to get wider and deeper. It creates a channel with banks on each side. What was once runoff is now a stream. Over hundreds of years, the stream can get large enough to form a river.

Down Under
A watershed is an area of land where surface water drains into a river, stream, or other body of water.

Where Rivers Meet

The place where streams or rivers meet one another is called a confluence. The word "confluence" comes from old Latin words that mean "flowing together."

Timing Water

Water moves at different speeds—even in the same section of a river. Water moves quickly in the center of a river channel and more slowly near its banks.

Rivers almost always travel downhill. Smaller streams, called tributaries, join larger rivers as the water flows downhill.

The path a river follows, or its course, can be quite a journey. The water in a river winds and snakes through hills and mountains. Then, it straightens as it reaches a plain. When the water tumbles over rapids, it fills with white bubbles and foam.

But as the course calms down, the water looks as smooth as glass.

Rivers change the land they flow through. Rushing water pulls at the sides and bottom of a river channel. Even solid rock erodes. Over time, erosion can carve narrow valleys with steep sides called canyons or gorges.

The Grand Canyon
It took the Colorado River and its tributaries between three and six million years to form Arizona's Grand Canyon. In some places, the canyon is 18 miles (29 km) wide and averages about a mile (1.6 km) deep.

Gorge or Canyon?
Gorges and canyons are similar, but they aren't exactly the same. Canyons are wider than gorges, and they are usually found in drier places.

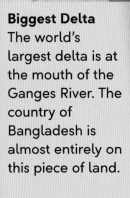

In some places, the land beneath a river gradually flattens. Here, the channel gets wider and wider, and the river's current, or the speed of its water, gets slower and slower. As the river ambles along, its course often forms big loops and bends. Fine soil, rocks, and silt—together called sediment—start to filter out of the slow-moving water.

A river's path ends at its mouth. The mouth is the point where a river empties into a larger body of water, such as another river or an ocean, lake, or sea. A river flows slower as it approaches its mouth.

This causes the sediment carried in the water to fall to the river's bottom. Over time, the sediment builds up to form a triangle-shaped piece of land called a delta at the river's mouth.

A delta's shape and size can change. When floods occur upstream, the water carries huge amounts of sediment. When this sediment is suddenly dropped at the river's mouth, the delta grows. A delta shrinks when a dam is built upstream. The dam can drastically reduce or even cut off the amount of water and sediment traveling to the river's mouth.

Big Bends
Bends in streams and rivers are called meanders.

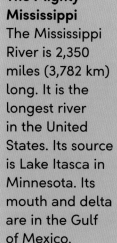

The Mighty Mississippi
The Mississippi River is 2,350 miles (3,782 km) long. It is the longest river in the United States. Its source is Lake Itasca in Minnesota. Its mouth and delta are in the Gulf of Mexico.

Big River, Big Watershed
The Amazon River's watershed covers about one-third of the entire continent of South America.

The Amazon River in South America and the Nile River in northern Africa are the world's largest rivers. Which is bigger? That depends on how you define "big"!

Before reaching the Atlantic Ocean, the Amazon River winds over 4,000 miles (6,400 km) through six countries in South America. The river has a fast current, and pounding ocean waves keep sediment from piling up. Because of this, the Amazon River has no delta.

Amazon River

The Amazon carries more water than any other river on the planet. Each day, enough water flows from the Amazon River into the Atlantic Ocean to supply the needs of New York City, New York, USA, for nearly a decade!

The Nile carries less water, but most people agree that it edges out the Amazon for length. This river is 4,100 miles (6,600 km) long. Between its source rivers in Burundi and Rwanda and its mouth at the Mediterranean Sea, the Nile travels through 11 African countries.

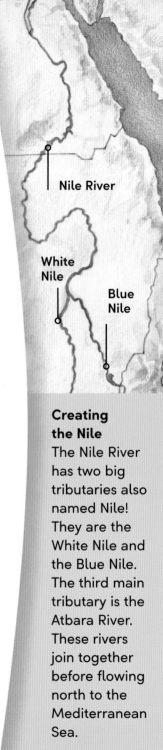

Nile River

White Nile

Blue Nile

Creating the Nile
The Nile River has two big tributaries also named Nile! They are the White Nile and the Blue Nile. The third main tributary is the Atbara River. These rivers join together before flowing north to the Mediterranean Sea.

Nile River

River currents can move fast. So, animals that live in and near rivers are good swimmers. Plants have adaptations that keep them from getting swept away in the swiftly moving water.

Places sheltered from the swiftest parts of rushing water make good habitats for whole communities of organisms.

Upstream Journey
Salmon spend much of their adult lives in the ocean. They return to the place in a river where they were born to lay their eggs. For some salmon, this means an upstream swim of hundreds of miles.

manatee

Plants can grow in a muddy river bottom. They provide shelter and food for small animals like salamanders. Fish with smooth, curved bodies, such as pike, are commonly found in rivers. Some fish, like salmon, are strong swimmers. Otters and mink live on riverbanks. Warmer rivers are home to even larger animals like manatees and dolphins.

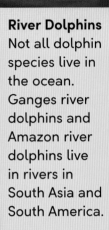

River Dolphins
Not all dolphin species live in the ocean. Ganges river dolphins and Amazon river dolphins live in rivers in South Asia and South America.

Flat Fish
Some fish, like catfish, live on river bottoms. Their bodies are flatter than those of other kinds of fish. Their shape allows the water to flow smoothly over the fish instead of pushing the fish along with the current.

Largest Lake
The Caspian Sea is actually a lake—the world's largest. Its water is saltier than most freshwater lakes but not as salty as the ocean.

Salt Lakes
Some lakes don't have an outlet. They only lose water through evaporation. Over time, these lakes become salty. The Great Salt Lake in the United States is much saltier than the ocean!

LAKES

Earth has over 100 million lakes. Like rivers, lakes are found on every continent and in every kind of environment, from hot deserts to cold mountaintops.

Unlike rivers, lakes are surrounded by land. Many lakes are fed by water from melting snow and ice. Most lakes have an outlet, which is a place where water leaves the lake. An outlet is usually a river or stream that flows on to join another larger body of water.

Most of the world's lakes are freshwater lakes. The water that fills them is sometimes so clear that you can see to the bottom of the lake.

But not all lakes are like this. And some, like Lake Natron in Tanzania, Africa, are downright toxic. This lake is so salty that most living things couldn't survive in its waters.

However, even here, there is life. Flamingos thrive in this salty environment. They have adaptations like thick, leathery skin on their legs and glands in their heads that remove salt from the near-boiling water they drink. These adaptations help them survive here.

Deepest Lake
Lake Baikal in Russia is over a mile (1.6 km) deep in some places. It holds almost as much water as the Great Lakes in North America combined.

What's a Pond?
A pond is a shallow lake. For a body of water to be called a pond, sunlight has to be able to reach its bottom.

Cirque Lakes
A cirque is a deep, steep basin carved by a glacier on a mountaintop. Lakes that fill these depressions are called cirque lakes.

Oxbow Lakes
Sometimes, sediment gathers at one end of a big bend, or meander, in a river. The bend is cut off from the rest of the river. The center of the loop floods with water, forming what's called an oxbow lake.

Lakes form in many different ways. Sometimes, a lake forms when the flow of a stream or river is stopped. Natural dams might occur when dirt and soil from a landslide blocks a river, or when beavers build a lodge on a stream.

Many lakes in North America are located in depressions, or basins. These low-lying areas were created when glaciers scraped large gouges in Earth's surface. When the glaciers melted, water filled the basins left behind, becoming lakes.

Crater Lake, Oregon, USA

Sometimes, when glaciers melted, they left enormous boulders of ice on a plain. The weight of the ice left deep pits in the land. Over time, melting ice and rainwater filled the pits, creating small, round lakes called kettle lakes.

Other lakes formed at the site of great faults and cracks in Earth's crust. Earth's deepest lake, Lake Baikal in Russia, formed this way. There are even lakes inside the craters of inactive volcanoes. Crater Lake in the United States is an example of this kind of lake.

Calderas
Volcanoes can erupt with such force that they blast holes in the sides of some mountains and cave in the tops of others. The depression left behind is called a caldera. Calderas can fill with water and become mountaintop lakes.

Lake Zones

The depth of a lake varies, depending on the landscape. Because of this, scientists divide lakes into zones. Each zone is based on how deep the water is at a certain point.

High or Low?

Plants and animals feed on nutrients found in lake waters. Lakes high in the mountains usually have fewer nutrients than lakes in other places. As a result, fewer kinds of plants and animals live in mountain lakes.

A lake's size can tell you a lot about conditions of the lake and its water.

Small lakes are warmer than larger ones. That's because sunlight shines on more of the water in a smaller lake. Smaller lakes are calmer. They don't usually have strong currents or large waves. The waves in large lakes can be as big as waves in the ocean. Earth's biggest lakes even have tides.

Turnover
In the spring and fall, lakes turn over—literally! The water at the top and bottom of the lake switches places. When this occurs, nutrients at the bottom of the lake move to the top. This is one reason why lakes are home to so many different kinds of plants and animals.

Lakes may last for hundreds of thousands of years, but even the biggest lakes are not permanent. Lakes have a life cycle. Young lakes sometimes get bigger, while old lakes get smaller. Over time, a lake's basin becomes shallower as it fills with the remains of dead plants and sediment washed in by rain. When the lake's water evaporates more quickly than it is replaced by precipitation, the lake shrinks. Eventually, the lake will disappear completely.

Another Great Lake

One of Africa's Great Lakes, Lake Victoria, is the second-largest freshwater lake on Earth. Multiple rivers from Uganda, Kenya, and Tanzania fill this lake. The lake has just one outlet, the Nile River.

HOMES

If you have trouble remembering the names of the Great Lakes in North America, just think of HOMES. Each letter is the first initial of one of the lakes: Huron, Ontario, Michigan, Erie, and Superior.

Lake Superior is the largest freshwater lake in the world, and it is part of the largest group of lakes, the Great Lakes. Glaciers formed these five lakes—Superior, Michigan, Huron, Ontario, and Erie—in North America over 10,000 years ago. The lakes contain about 20 percent of the world's fresh water. Three of the biggest freshwater lakes in the world are Great Lakes.

Because the Great Lakes are so large, they can impact the weather in the area around them.

This phenomenon is called the lake effect. The most famous result of the lake effect is snow—or rather, lots of snow! These massive snowfalls occur when cool air moves across warmer lake water in the winter. As the air absorbs heat from the water below, it picks up water that is evaporating from the lake. When this moist air rises and cools, the water comes down in blizzards of snow.

Naming the Great Lakes
Indigenous peoples were the first to name North America's Great Lakes. In their languages, Superior is *gichi-gami,* or "big water"; Huron is *karegnondi,* or "lake"; Erie is short for *erielhonan,* or "long tail"; Michigan is *mishigami,* or "great water"; and Ontario is *Oniatarí:io,* or "shining waters."

How Superior?
Lake Superior contains about half of the water in all of the Great Lakes.

Big Fish
Sturgeon can grow and grow and grow in their lake home! Lake sturgeons can grow up to nine feet (2.8 m) long and weigh up to 275 pounds (125 kg). Other sturgeon species grow much larger.

Many different kinds of plants and animals live in lakes. Warmer, shallow waters near a lake's shore often teem with small fish, frogs, and duckweed. Worms, insect larvae, and snapping turtles bury themselves in the muddy bottom near the shore, while lily pads float above. Bigger fish, like walleye and sturgeon, glide through deeper, colder waters. They feed on a layer of tiny aquatic organisms called plankton that float on the water's surface.

Many plants and animals live near lakes, too. Birds, such as kingfishers, osprey, and eagles, often sit in the branches of willow trees. They are keeping an eye out for fish. Muskrats, beavers, and mink build their homes in lakes or on lake shores. Bears sometimes live near lakes, too. A lake is a good place to find a steady supply of food and water.

Deepwater Dwellers
The deepest, darkest parts of lakes don't have a lot of life. Many of the animals that do live there, like mussels, snails, and leeches, spend their entire lives buried in the cold mud.

Finding Nutrients
The soil in bogs doesn't always contain a lot of nutrients. To survive in bogs, Venus flytraps and pitcher plants trap and digest insects. These plants get nutrients from their prey.

Peat Bogs
Peat looks like soil. It's not. It's a deposit of dead plants that are in the process of breaking down. Once peat is dried, it can be burned and used for fuel.

MARSHES

Marsh, bog, and swamp. They are all the same thing, right? Wrong! Each is a different type of wetland, and all of them are completely underwater for at least part of the year. Other than that, these areas have little in common.

Scientists categorize wetlands based on the kind of plants that grow in the area. If a wetland has a lot of bigger plants, such as trees and shrubs, it's almost definitely a swamp.

Bogs, on the other hand, are covered with a thick, carpet-like layer of moss.

Fast-growing plants like cattails and reeds are marsh plants. Their long, thin stems are flexible. So, these plants bend easily in the wind or with a current. Marshes are often found at the ends of lakes or at the mouths of rivers. Some marshes are right at the edge of the ocean.

Super Soggy Swamp
Plants don't breathe like animals do, but they still need air to survive. The ground in a swamp is always wet. Many of the trees and plants that grow there have adaptations that help the plants get the air they need to survive.

A marsh is an ever-changing environment. Some changes happen on a regular basis. For example, in spring, heavy rains and melting snow make the water in a marsh cold and deep. In winter, there is less precipitation, so the amount of dry land increases.

Other changes are sudden and have long-lasting effects. An upstream flood may wash a large amount of sediment into a marsh.

Estuaries
An estuary is a type of marsh found at the mouth of a river where it empties into the ocean. The water level and the amount of fresh or salty water in an estuary change with the tides.

Largest Marsh
Okavango Delta in Botswana, Africa, is one of the largest marshes in the world— about 2,300 square miles (6,000 sq km).

Dirt and rock get caught in the thick grasses and reeds. This creates more land and increases the size of the marsh.

Marshes act like natural filters in the environment. The plants and soil in a marsh soak up rainfall and keep land from flooding. They help filter out chemicals and pollution that might otherwise end up in lakes and oceans. In some places, marshes are even used to remove dirt and germs from household wastewater.

Tidal Marshes
Tidal marshes form along the edge of the ocean. The roots of grasses growing in these marshes help to hold the land in place, slowing erosion.

Big Predator
One of the largest predators in the United States, the Florida panther, lives in marshlands, including the Everglades.

An incredible variety of plants and animals lives in the world's marshlands. Thick grasses provide habitat for dragonflies and other insects. Amphibians, like salamanders and frogs, dine on these insects and their larvae. They lay their eggs in the shallow water. Many kinds of ducks, geese, and other waterfowl build nests in marshes, too. Cattails and reeds provide material to make nests, as well as lots of places to hide from predators.

Dragonflies
Dragonflies are really good at catching insects, including pesky mosquitoes. A dragonfly can catch and eat over hundreds of the biting insects in one day!

Floating Plants
Plants need light to grow. This can be a problem when the water level is constantly changing. Some marsh plants like bladderwort have air pockets inside their stems and leaves. These keep the plants afloat, close to the water's surface and the Sun.

The biggest marsh in the United States is the Everglades, in Florida. Sharp-bladed grasses, trees, wildflowers, and other plants cover more than 4,300 square miles (11,100 square km) in the southern part of the state. Raccoons, opossums, manatees, and alligators all make this wetland habitat their home. It is a protected environment where many rare and endangered species can survive.

RIVERS, LAKES, MARSHES ... AND PEOPLE!

Even if you don't live next to a river, lake, or marsh, you probably depend on one for comfort or even survival. People use these wetlands in many ways. They have for thousands of years!

About 8,000 years ago, ancient peoples in Egypt and Mesopotamia dug channels in the ground so water could flow from rivers into their fields. This is how they brought water to their crops.

Still Flowing
The Mississippi River carries about 500 million tons (454 million t) of goods every year.

Some of the most fertile farmland on Earth is found near rivers. When rivers flood, they drop sediment rich in nutrients on surrounding fields. This makes the land around rivers an excellent place to grow crops.

If you look at a map, you will find that many large cities around the world are located on the shores of rivers and lakes. Rivers and lakes were, and still are, an easy way to transport goods. They're the perfect place for people to relax, and they offer lots of different options for recreation.

Drinking Water
Over 100 million people in the United States get drinking water that originates in rivers.

Volta and Kariba
The two largest reservoirs in the world—both human-made—are in Africa. The biggest in area is Lake Volta, in Ghana. The reservoir that holds the most water, Lake Kariba, is between Zambia and Zimbabwe.

Ancient Technology
People have been building dams for at least 6,000 years.

Because lakes are such an important resource, people have built many lakes around the world. Almost half of the lakes in the US were created by people.

Artificial lakes are the by-product of human-made dams. Many artificial lakes are reservoirs. These are places where people store water to use for drinking and other purposes. They ensure that people will have enough water available, even during a drought.

Dams are useful for other reasons, too. During rainy seasons, people can open a dam so more water flows through. This helps to prevent flooding from the lake. During dry spells, a dam can be closed so less water flows through. This keeps the lake full and the water supply stable.

Hydropower
The water flow through some dams is used to generate electricity. Hydroelectric dams use the force of water to spin turbines. The turbines are connected to generators that make electricity.

Rice
Billions of people depend on rice as part of their diet. Rice is just one crop that grows in marshes and other wetlands.

Often, the way that people use rivers, lakes, and marshes can be harmful to wildlife. Marshes and other wetlands are especially at risk. Thousands of these areas have been drained of their water so that farms, homes, and businesses can be built on dry land. The pollution absorbed by wetlands is harmful to the ecosystem there, as well. As a result, many different kinds of plants and animals are in danger of becoming extinct.

Fortunately, people are taking action to preserve and protect marshes. They are repairing wetlands that have been damaged. They add soil and rock to the bottom of wetlands that have eroded. They replant reeds that have been removed. And people are completely rebuilding some marshes that have been drained.

Thanks to our understanding of how important rivers, lakes, and marshes are to people and to Earth, we will be able to enjoy them both now and in the future.

Restoration or Rehabilitation?
When people rebuild a marsh or other wetland that has been drained, the process is called restoration. If they fix one that has been damaged, the process is called rehabilitation.

GLOSSARY

Basin
A depression in the ground that becomes a lake when filled with water

Channel
A groove in the ground that forms a river's path

Condense
To change from a gas to a liquid

Evaporate
To change from a liquid to a gas

Erosion
The wearing away of Earth's surface by wind, water, or glacial ice

Fertile
Producing plants or crops

Fresh water
Water that has very little salt in it

Glacier
A slowly moving mass of ice

Hydrosphere
The scientific name for all of the water on Earth

Limnology
The study of Earth's fresh water

Meteorologist
A scientist who studies weather

Mouth
The place where a river empties into another body of water

Precipitation
Rain, snow, and other forms of water that fall from the sky

Source
The starting point of a river

Tributary
A smaller stream or river that flows into a larger one

Transpiration
The process in which water moves from plants into the atmosphere

Water vapor
Water in the form of a gas

INDEX

QUIZ

Answer the questions to see what you have learned. Check your answers in the key below.

1. How much of Earth's surface is covered with water?

2. True or False: Most of Earth's water is fresh water and in liquid form.

3. What is the beginning of a river called?

4. What is the speed of a river's water called?

5. Why is the Great Salt Lake so salty?

6. What is the name of the largest freshwater lake in the world?

7. True or False: Marsh, swamp, and bog are different names for the same thing.

8. What is the name of the biggest marsh in the United States?

1. About 70 percent 2. False 3. The source or headwater
4. The current 5. It has no outlet and only loses water
through evaporation 6. Lake Superior 7. False 8. The Everglades